The Play

A Division of The McGraw·Hill Companies

Columbus, Ohio

www.sra4kids.com

SRA/McGraw-Hill
A Division of The **McGraw·Hill** Companies

Copyright © 2002 by SRA/McGraw-Hill.

All rights reserved. Except as permitted under the United States Copyright Act, no part of this publication may be reproduced or distributed in any form or by any means, or stored in a database or retrieval system, without prior written permission from the publisher.

Printed in the United States of America.

Send all inquiries to:
SRA/McGraw-Hill
8787 Orion Place
Columbus, OH 43240-4027

ISBN 0-07-569744-0
 2 3 4 5 6 7 8 9 DBH 05 04 03 02

These belong to Eve.
Eve will use these.

"Here, Eve," said Steve. "These will make your clothing complete."

"Thank you, Steve," said Eve.
"These make me look even better."

Eve is acting in a play.
The theme of the play is fun, fun, fun.

Eve is acting with Pete.
Pete and Eve complete the play.

Eve and Pete are a big hit.